ANIMALS ON THE MOVE

IN THE AIR

WRITTEN BY
Eliza Nodes

PowerKiDS press

Published in 2026
by The Rosen Publishing Group, Inc.
2544 Clinton Street, Buffalo, NY 14224

Written by: Eliza Nodes
Edited by: Rebecca Phillips-Bartlett
Designed by: Rob Delph

All facts, statistics, web addresses, and URLs in this book were verified as valid and accurate at time of writing. No responsibility for any changes to external websites or references can be accepted by either the author or publisher.

Cataloging-in-Publication Data

Names: Nodes, Eliza.

Title: In the air / Eliza Nodes.

Description: Buffalo, New York : PowerKids Press, 2026. | Series: Animals on the move | Includes glossary and index.

Identifiers: ISBN 9781499455809 (pbk.) | ISBN 9781499455816 (library bound) | ISBN 9781499455823 (ebook)

Subjects: LCSH: Animal migration--Juvenile literature. | Animal behavior--Juvenile literature. | Adaption--Juvenile literature.

Classification: LCC QL754.N634 2026 | DDC 591.568--dc23

Printed in China

CPSIA Compliance Information: Batch #QW26PK. For further information contact Rosen Publishing at 1-800-237-9932.

PHOTO CREDITS

All images are courtesy of Shutterstock.com, unless otherwise stated. Front Cover – Independent birds, Ian Dewar Photography, Yulia Lakeienko, Georgi Baird. 2&3 – Roger de la Harpe, Ken Winkler. 4&5 – Daisy Salmon, Svetlana Pages, Victor1153, Knut Sandaker. 6&7 – Nancy Ann Bowe, GUDKOV ANDREY. 8&9 – Isabelle OHara, Escapist Indian. 10&11 – Ken Winkler, Rainer Lesniewski. 12&13 – Joel Trick, A Little Ray of Sunshine, JDzacovsky, John JonnyPink Knowles. 14&15 – Wirestock Creators, SJM51, Ken Griffiths. 16&17 – Neil Bowman, Imogen Warren. 18&19 – Richard Guijt Photography, Roger de la Harpe. 20&21 – ShadowHawk87, Carl Lorenz Overleashing. 22&23 – AJP, Chase D'animulls, Annmarie Young, Ken Griffiths, FRDMR.

CONTENTS

Words that look like this can be found in the glossary on page 24.

WHAT IS MIGRATION?

The movement of animals from place to place is called migration. Lots of animals, including birds, insects, and flying mammals, migrate through the skies. Some migrate more than once a year. Some are always on the move.

Mammals are warm-blooded animals that have a backbone and produce milk to feed their young.

Animal migrations happen for many reasons. Sometimes it is:

- Because of changes to their habitat
- To find food and water
- To find somewhere to have their young
- To avoid challenging weather

Let's have a look at some flying animals that migrate.

THE MONARCH BUTTERFLY FLUTTERS AWAY

Monarch butterflies fly between Mexico and the northern United States. They migrate for warmer weather and food. Four generations of butterflies are involved in the yearly migration cycle.

A generation is a group of animals who are roughly the same age.

Monarch butterflies leave Mexico in early spring. They lay eggs as they travel north. These eggs are the first generation.

It takes two more generations to reach their North American breeding grounds. The fourth and final generation is known as the super generation.

Every autumn, the super generation of monarch butterflies migrate over 2,485 miles (4,000 km) to Mexico. They do not stop to lay eggs on the way. They live much longer than the other generations.

No monarch butterflies survive the whole migration cycle. So, how do they know where to go and when to start traveling? Scientists have discovered that this is built into their bodies.

Their antennae tell the butterflies when to migrate.

THE HUMMINGBIRD'S AMERICAN TOUR

Many types of hummingbirds migrate. They travel from the southern United States to Mexico and Central America. This is so they can stay warm during winter and have plenty of nectar to eat.

Hummingbirds migrate alone. They can travel up to 500 miles (800 km) at a time.

Hummingbirds cross the Gulf of Mexico (sometimes called the Gulf of America). This is very tiring for them as there is no shelter or food there. Some hummingbirds do not survive.

A gulf is a large area of water partly surrounded by land.

Here are some ways you can help hummingbirds:

Plant flowers and hang feeders to give hummingbirds nectar to eat.

Provide perches where hummingbirds can rest during their long journey.

You can do these things whether you have a large garden or one outside flowerpot.

Put up window stickers to stop hummingbirds from flying into windows and doors.

Set up birdbaths to give hummingbirds water to drink and to keep them cool.

These things can help lots of different birds, not just hummingbirds.

THE FLOWERY FLIGHT OF THE LITTLE RED FLYING FOX

The little red flying fox is a type of bat that lives in Australia. They live in forest and woodland habitats. They roost in groups called camps. Camps can have up to a million bats.

Sometimes, tree branches break because so many bats roost on them.

Little red flying foxes are seasonal migrators. This means they migrate in summer and winter. They eat fruit and flowers. They migrate because there are more of these in warmer areas.

They are called flying foxes because their heads and faces look like a fox's.

Little red flying foxes are always on the move. They do not roost in the same place for longer than six weeks. Their endless traveling means they face lots of dangers caused by humans.

Their habitats are being cut down to clear land for farms and houses.

Little red flying foxes may take fruit from farms. Many farmers now think of them as pests. Some farmers hunt or poison flying foxes to stop them from eating their plants.

Little red flying foxes are good for forests. They spread fruit seeds and pollinate plants.

THE AFRICAN FLAMINGO'S SAFARI

Flamingos are well-known for their pink feathers and standing on one leg. There are two types of migratory flamingos in Africa. They are the lesser and greater flamingos.

A flamingo's ideal habitat is shallow water and wetland areas. This is because algae, the flamingo's favorite food, lives in these places. However, when the weather gets hotter, the wetlands can dry up.

Flamingos' feathers are pink because of the food they eat.

Flamingos migrate to find more food. However, they also migrate to another important place. They fly back to where they hatched as chicks. This is so they can have chicks of their own.

Flamingos usually stay away from other animals, so they do not have many predators. However, if predators are struggling, they may try to catch a flamingo. Flamingos migrate in groups to stay safe from attacks.

This hyena is tracking a flock of flamingos.

WHAT HAVE YOU LEARNED?

What can you remember about these flying animals that migrate? Let's do a quiz to find out! Make sure you have your paper and pencil ready to write down your answers.

QUESTIONS

1. How many generations are part of the yearly monarch butterfly migration cycle?

2. Do hummingbirds migrate in groups or on their own?

3. How did the little red flying fox get its name?

4. What are the names of the two types of flamingos in Africa?

Answers:

1. Four
2. On their own
3. Because its head and face look like a fox's
4. The greater and the lesser

GLOSSARY

ALGAE	a plantlike living thing that has no roots, stems, leaves, or flowers
ANTENNAE	a pair of long, thin sensors found on the heads of insects
BREEDING GROUNDS	the places where animals mate and produce their young
HABITAT	the natural home in which animals, plants, and other living things live
HATCHED	when a baby animal has come out of its egg
NECTAR	a sweet liquid made by plants
PESTS	creatures that damage things
POLLINATE	to pass on pollen from a plant to another plant of the same kind, so that seeds will be produced
PREDATORS	animals that hunt other animals for food
ROOST	when animals gather in groups to rest or sleep

INDEX